Aries 2025

Your Year in the Stars

Introduction

Welcome to "Aries 2025: Your Year in the Stars," your ultimate guide to navigating the celestial influences shaping your year ahead. As an Aries, born between March 21 and April 19, you embody a fiery spirit, boundless energy, and a pioneering nature. Your ruling planet, Mars, blesses you with courage, determination, and a relentless drive to conquer new frontiers. Your dynamic personality is often the catalyst for innovation and change, inspiring those around you to take bold steps.

In this book, we delve into each month of 2025, offering detailed horoscopes based on the timeless astrological techniques of Simon Forman. Forman's method, rooted in horary astrology, allows us to answer specific questions and predict events based on the positions of celestial bodies. Each chapter will provide you with insights and guidance to navigate the opportunities and challenges that lie ahead, helping you make the most of your Aries qualities.

January: Embracing New Beginnings

Overview

January marks a time of new beginnings, Aries. The year kicks off with a surge of energy, motivating you to set ambitious goals. With Mars, your ruling planet, transiting through Capricorn, you are driven to achieve professional success. This month, focus on strategic planning and laying the groundwork for future endeavors.

Key Dates

January 6: Full Moon in Cancer – Highlighting home and family matters.

January 13: Mars enters Aquarius – Encouraging innovation and social connections.

January 20: New Moon in Aquarius – A time for fresh starts in your social life and community involvement.

Detailed Horoscope

Full Moon in Cancer (January 6)

The Full Moon in Cancer on January 6 brings your attention to your domestic sphere. This lunar event highlights home and family matters, urging you to create a harmonious environment that supports your ambitions. You may find yourself resolving family issues or making decisions about your living arrangements. This is a time to nurture your emotional connections and strengthen your support network.

With the Full Moon illuminating your fourth house of home and family, you are encouraged to address any imbalances in your domestic life. If you have been neglecting your home or family due to work commitments, now is the time to restore balance. Consider spending quality time with loved ones, engaging in family activities, or making improvements to your living space. Your efforts to create a peaceful and nurturing home environment will pay off in the long run.

Mars Enters Aquarius (January 13)

On January 13, Mars enters Aquarius, shifting your focus to networking and collaboration. This transit encourages you to embrace innovation and think outside the box. You may find yourself drawn to new social circles or community projects that align with your goals. Your leadership qualities will shine, making you a magnet for those seeking inspiration.

Mars in Aquarius energizes your eleventh house of friendships and social networks. This is an excellent time to expand your social circle and connect with like-minded individuals who share your vision. Consider joining groups or organizations that align with your interests and values. Your ability to inspire and motivate others will help you build strong, supportive relationships that can advance your goals.

New Moon in Aquarius (January 20)

The New Moon on January 20 offers a fresh start in your social life. This is a powerful time for setting new intentions and launching new initiatives. Whether it's joining a new group, starting a community project, or expanding your network, this New Moon supports your efforts to connect with others and make a positive impact.

The New Moon in Aquarius activates your eleventh house of friendships and community. This is a time to plant seeds for future growth and collaboration. Consider setting goals related to your social life, such as building new friendships, enhancing existing relationships, or participating in community activities. Your innovative ideas and visionary thinking will help you attract the right people and opportunities to support your aspirations.

Practical Tips for January

Set Clear Goals: Use the energy of the New Year to set clear, ambitious goals for the year ahead. Break them down into manageable steps and create a strategic plan to achieve them.

Balance Work and Home: Ensure you maintain a healthy balance between your professional and personal life. Dedicate time to nurture your relationships in order to create a warm and harmonious home environment.

Embrace Innovation: Be open to new ideas and innovative solutions. Join groups or communities that can serve to inspire you and support your goals.

Nurture Your Network: Strengthen your social connections by reaching out to friends, joining new groups, and participating in community activities. Your ability to inspire others will help you build a strong support network.

February: Building Momentum

Overview

February is a month of steady progress, Aries. The groundwork you laid in January begins to yield results. With Venus in Pisces, there is a focus on creativity and emotional fulfillment. This is a time to nurture your passions and strengthen your relationships.

Key Dates

February 5: Full Moon in Leo – Illuminating creative projects and romantic endeavors.

February 11: Venus enters Aries – Enhancing your charm and attractiveness.

February 19: New Moon in Pisces – A time for introspection and spiritual growth.

Detailed Horoscope

Full Moon in Leo (February 5)

The Full Moon in Leo on February 5 brings your creative talents to the forefront. This lunar event highlights your fifth house of creativity, romance, and self-expression. You are encouraged to showcase your talents, whether it's through a project at work or a personal hobby. This is a time to let your inner light shine and embrace your unique gifts.

With the Full Moon illuminating your fifth house, your romantic relationships are also highlighted. You may experience a deeper connection with your partner, or new romantic opportunities may arise. This is a time to embrace joy and passion in your relationships, allowing your heart to guide you.

If you have been working on a creative project, the Full Moon in Leo provides the perfect opportunity to present your work to the world. Whether it's an art piece, a business proposal, or a personal endeavor, your efforts are likely to be met with admiration and appreciation. Use this energy to celebrate your achievements and inspire others with your creativity.

Venus Enters Aries (February 11)

Venus enters Aries on February 11, boosting your confidence and allure. This transit enhances your charm and attractiveness, making you more appealing to others. You may find yourself receiving more attention and admiration, both personally and professionally. This is a great time to start new romantic relationships or rekindle the spark in existing ones.

Venus in Aries activates your first house of self and identity. You are encouraged to embrace your individuality and express your unique qualities. Your natural charisma and charm will attract positive attention, helping you build meaningful connections. This is also a good time to indulge in self-care and enhance your appearance.

New Moon in Pisces (February 19)

The New Moon on February 19 encourages introspection and spiritual growth. This lunar event activates your twelfth house of spirituality and subconscious. It's a time to reflect on your goals, connect with your inner self, and engage in practices that nurture your soul. Meditation, journaling, and other spiritual practices can provide valuable insights and help you gain clarity.

The New Moon in Pisces offers a fresh start for your inner journey. Consider setting intentions related to your spiritual growth, emotional healing, and personal development. This is a time to release any emotional baggage and embrace a more peaceful and harmonious state of mind.

Practical Tips for February

Showcase Your Talents: Use the energy of the Full Moon in Leo to present your creative projects and embrace your unique gifts. Your efforts will be met with admiration and appreciation.

Embrace Romance: Strengthen your romantic relationships by expressing your love and passion. New romantic opportunities may arise, so be open to making new connections and seeking fresh opportunities.

Boost Your Confidence: With Venus in Aries, focus on enhancing your appearance and embracing your individuality. Your natural charm and charisma will come bursting out and attract the most positive sort of attention.

Engage in Spiritual Practices: Use the energy of the New Moon in Pisces to reflect on your goals and connect with your inner self. Meditation, journaling, and other spiritual practices can provide valuable insights.

March: Taking Bold Steps

Overview

March is a dynamic month for you, Aries. With the Sun entering your sign, your vitality and confidence are at their peak. This is a time to take bold steps towards your goals and assert your independence.

Key Dates

March 7: Full Moon in Virgo – Highlighting health and daily routines.

March 20: The Sun enters Aries – Marking the start of your solar return.

March 28: New Moon in Aries – A powerful time for setting intentions and new beginnings.

Detailed Horoscope

Full Moon in Virgo (March 7)

The Full Moon in Virgo on March 7 shines a light on your health and daily routines. This lunar event activates your sixth house of wellness, urging you to assess your habits and make necessary changes to improve your well-being. Consider adopting a new exercise regimen, refining your diet, or incorporating mindfulness practices into your daily routine.

With the Full Moon illuminating your sixth house, you are encouraged to focus on your physical and mental health. If you have been neglecting your well-being due to a busy schedule, now is the time to restore balance. Consider seeking professional advice or support to help you achieve your health goals.

The Full Moon in Virgo also highlights your daily routines and work environment. You may find yourself addressing any inefficiencies or imbalances in your workflow. This is a good time to organize your workspace, streamline your tasks, and create a more productive and harmonious environment.

Sun Enters Aries (March 20)

The Sun enters Aries on March 20, marking the start of your solar return. This transit boosts your energy and confidence, making you more assertive and ready to take on new challenges. Your leadership qualities are emphasized, and you may find yourself stepping into a prominent role.

With the Sun in your first house of self and identity, you are encouraged to embrace your individuality and assert your independence. This is a time to focus on your personal goals and take bold steps towards achieving them. Your natural charisma and confidence will help you attract positive attention and support from others.

The Sun's transit through Aries also highlights your physical vitality and appearance. This is a good time to focus on self-care and enhance your overall well-being. Consider adopting new fitness routines, updating your wardrobe, or making changes that boost your confidence.

New Moon in Aries (March 28)

The New Moon on March 28 offers a powerful time for setting intentions and new beginnings. This lunar event activates your first house of self and identity, providing a fresh start for your personal goals and aspirations. Use this energy to set clear intentions and take bold steps towards manifesting your dreams.

The New Moon in Aries encourages you to embrace your individuality and assert your independence. This is a time to focus on what you truly desire and take proactive steps to achieve your goals. Consider setting intentions related to your personal growth, career ambitions, and overall well-being.

Practical Tips for March

Focus on Wellness: Use the energy of the Full Moon in Virgo to assess your health and daily routines. Make necessary changes to improve your well-being and achieve a more balanced, harmonious and rewarding lifestyle.

Embrace Leadership: With the Sun in Aries, step into a leadership role and assert your independence. Focus on your goals and take bold steps towards achieving them.

Set Intentions: Use the energy of the New Moon in Aries to set clear intentions and take proactive steps towards manifesting your dreams. Embrace your individuality, assert your independence and get ready to reap the rewards.

Enhance Your Appearance: Focus on self-care and enhance your overall well-being. Consider adopting new fitness routines, updating your wardrobe, or making changes that boost your confidence.

April: Nurturing Relationships

Overview

April is a month to focus on relationships, both personal and professional. With Venus in Taurus, there is an emphasis on stability and security. This is a time to nurture your connections and build a strong support network.

Key Dates

April 6: Full Moon in Libra – Highlighting partnerships and balance.

April 14: Venus enters Gemini – Encouraging communication and intellectual connections.

April 27: New Moon in Taurus – A time for financial planning and stability.

Detailed Horoscope

Full Moon in Libra (April 6)

The Full Moon in Libra on April 6 illuminates your partnerships. This lunar event activates your seventh house of relationships, urging you to address any imbalances and work towards harmony. Whether it's a romantic partner, a business associate, or a close friend, clear communication and mutual understanding are key.

With the Full Moon illuminating your seventh house, you are encouraged to focus on your one-on-one relationships. If there have been any unresolved issues or conflicts, now is the time to address them. Consider having open and honest conversations with your partner or seeking the help of a mediator if needed.

The Full Moon in Libra also highlights the importance of balance and fairness in your relationships. You may find yourself reassessing the give-and-take dynamics in your partnerships. Strive for mutual respect and understanding, ensuring that both parties feel valued and heard.

Venus Enters Gemini (April 14)

Venus enters Gemini on April 14, bringing a focus on communication and intellectual connections. This transit enhances your social skills and encourages you to engage in meaningful conversations. You may find yourself drawn to stimulating discussions and activities that broaden your horizons.

Venus in Gemini activates your third house of communication and learning. This is a time to strengthen your social network and connect with people who inspire you. Consider joining groups or participating in activities that align with your interests. Your ability to articulate your ideas and express your thoughts will help you build strong connections.

The transit of Venus through Gemini also encourages you to embrace curiosity and learning. You may find yourself drawn to new studies, hobbies, or intellectual pursuits. This is a good time to expand your knowledge and engage in activities that stimulate your mind.

New Moon in Taurus (April 27)

The New Moon on April 27 is a time for financial planning and stability. This lunar event activates your second house of resources, urging you to focus on your financial goals and create a solid foundation for your future. Consider setting practical goals to secure your financial future and make wise investments.

With the New Moon illuminating your second house, you are encouraged to take a practical approach to your finances. This is a time to assess your financial situation, create a budget, and set clear goals for your financial growth. Consider seeking professional advice or exploring new investment opportunities to enhance your financial stability.

The New Moon in Taurus also encourages you to indulge in self-care and enjoy the finer things in life. Consider treating yourself to something special or engaging in activities that bring you joy and relaxation. By nurturing yourself, you will be better equipped to achieve your financial goals and create a balanced and fulfilling life.

Practical Tips for April

Focus on Relationships: Use the energy of the Full Moon in Libra to address any imbalances in your partnerships. Clear communication and mutual understanding are key to creating harmony.

Enhance Communication: With Venus in Gemini, focus on strengthening your social network and engaging in meaningful conversations. Embrace your curiosity and seek opportunities that will enhance your knowledge.

Financial Planning: Use the energy of the New Moon in Taurus to set practical financial goals and create a solid foundation for your future. Consider seeking professional advice or exploring new investment opportunities.

Indulge in Self-Care: Take time to nurture yourself and enjoy the finer things in life. By prioritizing self-care, you will be better equipped to achieve your financial and personal goals.

May: Embracing Change

Overview

May brings opportunities for growth and transformation, Aries. With Jupiter entering Taurus, there is a focus on expanding your horizons and embracing new experiences. This is a time to step out of your comfort zone and explore new possibilities.

Key Dates

May 5: Full Moon in Scorpio – Highlighting shared resources and transformation.

May 11: Jupiter enters Taurus – Encouraging growth and expansion.

May 25: New Moon in Gemini – A time for learning and communication.

Detailed Horoscope

Full Moon in Scorpio (May 5)

The Full Moon in Scorpio on May 5 highlights shared resources and transformation. This lunar event activates your eighth house of intimacy and shared finances, urging you to address any financial matters involving others. Whether it's joint accounts, investments, or debts, now is the time to take a closer look and make necessary adjustments.

With the Full Moon illuminating your eighth house, you are encouraged to embrace deep personal transformation. This is a time to release any emotional baggage and let go of what no longer serves you. Consider engaging in practices that promote emotional healing and self-discovery, such as therapy, meditation, or journaling.

The Full Moon in Scorpio also highlights the importance of trust and intimacy in your relationships. You may find yourself reassessing the dynamics of your close partnerships and addressing any issues related to power, control, or vulnerability. Strive for honesty and transparency in your interactions, fostering a deeper sense of connection and mutual understanding.

Jupiter Enters Taurus (May 11)

Jupiter enters Taurus on May 11, bringing opportunities for growth and expansion. This transit activates your second house of resources, encouraging you to explore new ways to enhance your financial stability and create abundance. You may find yourself drawn to new studies, travel, or professional opportunities that broaden your horizons.

Jupiter in Taurus encourages you to take a practical and grounded approach to your goals. This is a time to focus on building a solid foundation for your future, whether it's through financial planning, investing in new skills, or pursuing higher education. Your efforts to expand your knowledge and resources will pay off in the long run.

The transit of Jupiter through Taurus also encourages you to embrace a sense of gratitude and abundance. By focusing on what you have and appreciating the blessings in your life, you will attract more opportunities for growth and prosperity. Consider adopting practices that cultivate a positive mindset, such as gratitude journaling or mindfulness meditation.

New Moon in Gemini (May 25)

The New Moon on May 25 is a time for learning and communication. This lunar event activates your third house of communication and learning, encouraging you to set new intentions related to your intellectual growth and social interactions. Whether it's starting a new course, engaging in stimulating discussions, or sharing your knowledge with others, this New Moon supports your efforts to expand your mind and connect with others.

With the New Moon illuminating your third house, you are encouraged to embrace curiosity and explore new ideas. Consider setting goals related to your intellectual pursuits, such as learning a new language, taking up a new hobby, or engaging in activities that stimulate your mind. Your natural curiosity and thirst for knowledge will help you expand your horizons and discover new possibilities.

The New Moon in Gemini also highlights the importance of effective communication. This is a time to refine your communication skills and express your ideas with clarity and confidence. Consider engaging in activities that enhance your communication abilities, such as writing, public speaking, or networking.

Practical Tips for May

Address Financial Matters: Use the energy of the Full Moon in Scorpio to take a closer look at your shared resources and make necessary adjustments. Focus on trust and transparency in your financial and personal relationships.

Embrace Growth: With Jupiter in Taurus, focus on building a solid foundation for your future. Explore new opportunities for learning, travel, and professional growth to enhance your financial stability and create abundance.

Set Learning Goals: Use the energy of the New Moon in Gemini to set new intentions related to your intellectual growth and social interactions. Embrace curiosity and explore new ideas to expand your mind and connect with others.

Enhance Communication: Focus on refining your communication skills and expressing your ideas with clarity and confidence

Engage in activities that enhance your communication abilities and help you connect with others.

June: Expanding Horizons

Overview

June is a month of exploration and adventure, Aries. With Mars in Leo, there is a focus on creativity and self-expression. This is a time to embrace your passions and pursue new experiences.

Key Dates

June 4: Full Moon in Sagittarius – Highlighting travel and higher learning.

June 11: Mars enters Leo – Encouraging creativity and self-expression.

June 18: New Moon in Cancer – A time for emotional growth and nurturing relationships.

Detailed Horoscope

Full Moon in Sagittarius (June 4)

The Full Moon in Sagittarius on June 4 highlights travel and higher learning. This lunar event activates your ninth house of exploration, urging you to step out of your comfort zone and embrace new experiences. Whether it's planning a trip, pursuing higher education, or exploring new philosophies, now is the time to broaden your horizons.

With the Full Moon illuminating your ninth house, you are encouraged to seek adventure and expand your knowledge. Consider engaging in activities that challenge your beliefs and open your mind to new perspectives. This is a time to embrace the unknown and explore new possibilities.

The Full Moon in Sagittarius also highlights the importance of personal growth and self-discovery. You may find yourself reassessing your beliefs and values, seeking deeper meaning and purpose in your life. Embrace opportunities for spiritual growth and self-reflection, allowing yourself to grow and evolve.

Mars Enters Leo (June 11)

Mars enters Leo on June 11, bringing a focus on creativity and self-expression. This transit activates your fifth house of creativity, romance, and self-expression, encouraging you to embrace your passions and pursue activities that bring you joy. Whether it's through artistic endeavors, romantic relationships, or playful activities, now is the time to let your inner light shine.

Mars in Leo energizes your creative endeavors and encourages you to take bold steps towards your goals. This is a time to showcase your talents and express your unique gifts. Consider engaging in activities that allow you to express yourself, such as art, music, or theater. Your natural charisma and confidence will help you attract positive attention and support from others.

The transit of Mars through Leo also highlights the importance of joy and playfulness in your life. Consider engaging in activities that bring you happiness and allow you to connect with your inner child. By embracing a sense of play and spontaneity, you will enhance your overall well-being and create a more fulfilling life.

New Moon in Cancer (June 18)

The New Moon on June 18 is a time for emotional growth and nurturing relationships. This lunar event activates your fourth house of home and family, encouraging you to focus on your emotional well-being and create a harmonious home environment. Consider setting new intentions related to your family life, emotional healing, and personal growth.

With the New Moon illuminating your fourth house, you are encouraged to nurture your emotional connections and create a supportive home environment. Consider spending quality time with loved ones, engaging in family activities, or making improvements to your living space. Your efforts to create a peaceful and nurturing home environment will pay off in the long run.

The New Moon in Cancer also encourages you to focus on your emotional well-being. Consider engaging in practices that promote emotional healing and self-care, such as therapy, meditation, or journaling. By nurturing your emotional health, you will enhance your overall well-being and create a more balanced and fulfilling life.

Practical Tips for June

Embrace Adventure: Use the energy of the Full Moon in Sagittarius to step out of your comfort zone and embrace new experiences. Explore new possibilities and seek adventure.

June will be the ideal time to broaden your horizons.

Showcase Your Talents: With Mars in Leo, focus on your creative endeavors and express your unique gifts. Engage in activities that allow you to showcase your wealth of talents and attract positive attention.

Nurture Relationships: Use the energy of the New Moon in Cancer to focus on your emotional connections and create a supportive home environment.

Spend quality time with loved ones and engage in activities that contribute to your sense of emotional well-being.

Focus on Emotional Growth: Engage in practices that promote emotional healing and self-care. Nurture your emotional health to enhance your overall well-being and create a more balanced and fulfilling life.

July: Strengthening Foundations

Overview

July is a month to focus on strengthening your foundations, Aries. With the Sun in Cancer, there is an emphasis on home and family. This is a time to create a solid foundation for your future and nurture your emotional well-being.

Key Dates

July 3: Full Moon in Capricorn – Highlighting career and long-term goals.

July 10: Mercury enters Leo – Encouraging creative communication.

July 24: New Moon in Leo – A time for creative projects and self-expression.

Detailed Horoscope

Full Moon in Capricorn (July 3)

The Full Moon in Capricorn on July 3 highlights your career and long-term goals. This lunar event activates your tenth house of career and public life, urging you to assess your professional ambitions and make necessary adjustments to achieve your goals. Consider taking a closer look at your career path and making changes to enhance your professional growth.

With the Full Moon illuminating your tenth house, you are encouraged to focus on your long-term goals and aspirations. This is a time to set clear, ambitious goals for your career and take proactive steps towards achieving them. Consider seeking professional advice or exploring new opportunities for growth and advancement.

The Full Moon in Capricorn also highlights the importance of balance and structure in your professional life. You may find yourself reassessing your work-life balance and making necessary adjustments to create a more harmonious and fulfilling career. Strive for a balance between your professional ambitions and personal well-being.

Mercury Enters Leo (July 10)

Mercury enters Leo on July 10, bringing a focus on creative communication. This transit activates your fifth house of creativity and self-expression, encouraging you to express your ideas with confidence and clarity. Whether it's through writing, speaking, or artistic endeavors, now is the time to showcase your talents and share your unique perspective.

Mercury in Leo enhances your communication skills and encourages you to engage in meaningful conversations. This is a time to articulate your ideas and express your thoughts with clarity and confidence. Consider engaging in activities that allow you to showcase your creative talents, such as writing, public speaking, or networking.

The transit of Mercury through Leo also highlights the importance of self-expression and creativity in your life. Consider engaging in activities that allow you to express yourself, such as art, music, or theater. Your natural charisma and confidence will help you attract positive attention and support from others.

New Moon in Leo (July 24)

The New Moon on July 24 is a time for creative projects and self-expression. This lunar event activates your fifth house of creativity, romance, and self-expression, providing a fresh start for your creative endeavors and personal goals. Use this energy to set new intentions and take bold steps towards manifesting your dreams.

With the New Moon illuminating your fifth house, you are encouraged to embrace your passions and pursue activities that bring you joy. Consider setting goals related to your creative projects, romantic relationships, and personal growth. Your natural creativity and confidence will help you attract positive attention and support from others.

The New Moon in Leo also highlights the importance of joy and playfulness in your life. Consider engaging in activities that bring you happiness and allow you to connect with your inner child. By embracing a sense of play and spontaneity, you will enhance your overall well-being and create a more fulfilling life.

Practical Tips for July

Focus on Career Goals: Use the energy of the Full Moon in Capricorn to assess your professional ambitions and make necessary adjustments to achieve your goals. Strive for balance and structure in your professional   life.

Enhance Communication: With Mercury in Leo, focus on expressing your ideas with confidence and clarity.

Engage in activities that allow you to showcase your creative talents and share your unique perspective.

Set Creative Goals: Use the energy of the New Moon in Leo to set new intentions for your creative projects and personal goals. Embrace your passions, focus on those activities that bring you joy, and allow yourself to shine.

Embrace Playfulness: Engage in activities that bring you happiness and allow you to connect with your inner child. By embracing a sense of play and spontaneity, you will enhance your overall well-being and create a more fulfilling life.

August: Embracing Opportunities

Overview

August brings opportunities for growth and expansion, Aries. With the Sun in Leo, there is a focus on creativity and self-expression. This is a time to embrace new experiences and pursue your passions.

Key Dates

August 1: Full Moon in Aquarius – Highlighting social connections and community involvement.

August 10: Venus enters Virgo – Encouraging attention to detail and practicality.

August 23: New Moon in Virgo – A time for health and wellness goals.

Detailed Horoscope

The Full Moon in Aquarius on August 1 highlights your social connections and community involvement. This lunar event activates your eleventh house of friendships and social networks, urging you to strengthen your relationships and engage in activities that align with your values. Whether it's joining a new group, participating in community events, or reconnecting with old friends, now is the time to expand your social circle.

With the Full Moon illuminating your eleventh house, you are encouraged to focus on your social connections and community involvement. Consider reaching out to friends, joining new groups, or participating in activities that align with your interests and values. Your ability to inspire and motivate others will help you build strong, supportive relationships.

The Full Moon in Aquarius also highlights the importance of collaboration and teamwork in achieving your goals. You may find yourself working on group projects or community initiatives that require cooperation and mutual support. Strive for a balance between your individual goals and the collective needs of your community.

Venus Enters Virgo (August 10)

Venus enters Virgo on August 10, bringing a focus on attention to detail and practicality. This transit activates your sixth house of health and daily routines, encouraging you to take a practical approach to your well-being and create healthy habits. Whether it's through diet, exercise, or self-care routines, now is the time to prioritize your health and create a balanced lifestyle.

Venus in Virgo enhances your ability to focus on the details and create practical solutions. This is a time to assess your daily routines and make necessary adjustments to improve your overall well-being. Consider adopting new habits that support your health and create a sense of balance and harmony in your life.

The transit of Venus through Virgo also highlights the importance of self-care and attention to detail in your relationships. Consider engaging in activities that enhance your well-being and create a sense of balance and harmony in your life. By prioritizing self-care, you will enhance your overall well-being and create more fulfilling relationships.

New Moon in Virgo (August 23)

The New Moon on August 23 is a time for health and wellness goals. This lunar event activates your sixth house of health and daily routines, providing a fresh start for your well-being and personal growth. Use this energy to set new intentions and take proactive steps towards achieving your health and wellness goals.

With the New Moon illuminating your sixth house, you are encouraged to focus on your health and create a balanced lifestyle. Consider setting goals related to your diet, exercise, and self-care routines. Your efforts to prioritize your well-being will pay off in the long run, enhancing your overall health and vitality.

The New Moon in Virgo also highlights the importance of practicality and attention to detail in achieving your goals. Consider creating a detailed plan and taking practical steps towards achieving your health and wellness goals. By focusing on the details and staying organized, you will enhance your overall well-being and create a more balanced and fulfilling life.

Practical Tips for August

Strengthen Social Connections: Use the energy of the Full Moon in Aquarius to focus on your social connections and community involvement. August will be the perfect time to engage in activities that align with your interests and values to build strong, supportive relationships.

Prioritize health. With Venus in Virgo, focus on creating healthy habits and a balanced lifestyle. Assess your daily routines and make necessary adjustments to improve your overall well-being. Minor adjustments can lead to major changes, and there is no better time to start.

Create a detailed plan and take practical steps towards achieving your health goals this month, Venus will offer all the help you need and the journey will be simpler and more enjoyable than you may have expected.

Embrace Practicality: Focus on attention to detail and practicality in achieving your goals. By staying organized and focused, you will enhance your overall well-being and create a more balanced and fulfilling life.

September: Pursuing Goals

Overview

September is a month to focus on pursuing your goals, Aries. With the Sun in Virgo, there is an emphasis on health and daily routines. This is a time to create a solid foundation for your future and achieve your personal and professional ambitions.

Key Dates

September 2: Full Moon in Pisces – Highlighting spirituality and emotional well-being.

September 9: Mars enters Libra – Encouraging balance and harmony in relationships.

September 17: New Moon in Libra – A time for new beginnings in relationships and partnerships.

Detailed Horoscope

Full Moon in Pisces (September 2)

The Full Moon in Pisces on September 2 highlights your spirituality and emotional well-being. This lunar event activates your twelfth house of spirituality and inner growth, urging you to focus on your emotional health and spiritual practices. Consider engaging in activities that promote emotional healing and self-discovery, such as therapy, meditation, or journaling.

With the Full Moon illuminating your twelfth house, you are encouraged to embrace your inner world and focus on your emotional well-being. Consider setting aside time for introspection and self-reflection, allowing yourself to connect with your inner self. This is a time to release any emotional baggage and let go of what no longer serves you.

The Full Moon in Pisces also highlights the importance of compassion and empathy in your interactions with others. Consider engaging in activities that promote emotional healing and self-discovery, such as therapy, meditation, or journaling. Your ability to connect with others on a deeper level will enhance your relationships and create a sense of emotional well-being.

Mars Enters Libra (September 9)

Mars enters Libra on September 9, bringing a focus on balance and harmony in relationships. This transit activates your seventh house of partnerships, encouraging you to work towards creating harmony and mutual understanding in your relationships. Whether it's a romantic partner, a business associate, or a close friend, now is the time to focus on balance and cooperation.

Mars in Libra enhances your ability to work towards balance and harmony in your relationships. This is a time to address any imbalances and work towards creating mutual understanding and respect. Consider engaging in activities that promote cooperation and teamwork, such as joint projects or collaborative efforts.

The transit of Mars through Libra also highlights the importance of compromise and cooperation in achieving your goals. Consider seeking the help of a mediator or counselor if needed, and strive for a balance between your individual needs and the needs of your partner. By working together, you will create stronger, more fulfilling relationships.

New Moon in Libra (September 17)

The New Moon on September 17 is a time for new beginnings in relationships and partnerships. This lunar event activates your seventh house of partnerships, providing a fresh start for your relationships and personal goals. Use this energy to set new intentions and take proactive steps towards achieving harmony and mutual understanding in your partnerships.

With the New Moon illuminating your seventh house, you are encouraged to focus on creating balance and harmony in your relationships. Consider setting new intentions related to your partnerships, whether it's a romantic relationship, a business partnership, or a close friendship. Your efforts to create mutual understanding and respect will pay off in the long run.

The New Moon in Libra also highlights the importance of cooperation and teamwork in achieving your goals. Consider engaging in activities that promote harmony and mutual understanding, such as joint projects or collaborative efforts. By working together, you will create stronger, more fulfilling relationships and achieve your personal and professional ambitions.

Practical Tips for September

Focus on Emotional Well-Being: Use the energy of the Full Moon in Pisces to focus on your emotional health and spiritual practices.

Engage in activities that promote emotional healing and self-discovery.

Create Balance: With Mars in Libra, focus on creating balance and harmony in your relationships. Address any imbalances and work towards mutual understanding and respect.

Set Relationship Goals: Use the energy of the New Moon in Libra to set new intentions for your relationships and partnerships. Focus on creating harmony and mutual understanding in your interactions with others.

Engage in Cooperation: Consider engaging in activities that promote cooperation and teamwork. By working together, you will create stronger, more fulfilling relationships and achieve your personal and professional goals.

October: Embracing Transformation

Overview

October brings opportunities for transformation and renewal, Aries. With the Sun in Scorpio, there is a focus on deep emotional healing and personal growth. This is a time to embrace change and let go of what no longer serves you.

Key Dates

October 1: Full Moon in Aries – Highlighting personal goals and self-identity.

October 10: Mercury enters Scorpio – Encouraging deep communication and introspection.

October 25: New Moon in Scorpio – A time for transformation and renewal.

Detailed Horoscope

Full Moon in Aries (October 1)

The Full Moon in Aries on October 1 highlights your personal goals and self-identity. This lunar event activates your first house of self and identity, urging you to focus on your personal ambitions and take proactive steps towards achieving your goals. Consider taking a closer look at your personal path and making necessary adjustments to enhance your personal growth.

With the Full Moon illuminating your first house, you are encouraged to embrace your individuality and assert your independence. Consider setting clear, ambitious goals for your personal growth and taking bold steps towards achieving them. Your natural confidence and determination will help you attract positive attention and support from others.

The Full Moon in Aries also highlights the importance of self-care and self-expression. You may find yourself reassessing your personal goals and making necessary adjustments to create a more fulfilling and balanced life. Strive for a balance between your personal ambitions and your overall well-being.

Mercury enters Scorpio on October 10, bringing a focus on deep communication and introspection. This transit activates your eighth house of intimacy and shared resources, encouraging you to engage in meaningful conversations and explore your inner world. Whether it's through deep discussions with a partner, therapy, or journaling, now is the time to connect with your inner self and others on a deeper level.

Mercury in Scorpio enhances your ability to communicate with depth and authenticity. This is a time to engage in meaningful conversations and explore your inner world. Consider engaging in activities that promote emotional healing and self-discovery, such as therapy, meditation, or journaling.

The transit of Mercury through Scorpio also highlights the importance of honesty and transparency in your interactions with others. Consider addressing any unresolved issues or conflicts in your relationships and striving for mutual understanding and respect. By connecting with others on a deeper level, you will enhance your relationships and create a sense of emotional well-being.

New Moon in Scorpio (October 25)

The New Moon on October 25 is a time for transformation and renewal. This lunar event activates your eighth house of intimacy and shared resources, providing a fresh start for your personal growth and emotional healing. Use this energy to set new intentions and take proactive steps towards embracing change and letting go of what no longer serves you.

With the New Moon illuminating your eighth house, you are encouraged to embrace deep personal transformation. Consider setting new intentions related to your emotional healing, personal growth, and shared resources. Your efforts to embrace change and let go of what no longer serves you will pay off in the long run, enhancing your overall well-being.

The New Moon in Scorpio also highlights the importance of emotional healing and personal growth. Consider engaging in activities that promote emotional healing and self-discovery, such as therapy, meditation, or journaling. By focusing on your emotional well-being, you will enhance your overall health and create a more balanced and fulfilling life.

Practical Tips for October

Focus on Personal Goals: Use the energy of the Full Moon in Aries to focus on your personal ambitions and take proactive steps towards achieving your goals. Embrace your individuality and assert your independence.

Engage in Deep Communication: With Mercury in Scorpio, focus on engaging in meaningful conversations and exploring your inner world. Address any unresolved issues or conflicts in your relationships and strive for mutual understanding and respect. Honesty will pay dividends.

Embrace Transformation: Use the energy of the New Moon in Scorpio to set new intentions for your personal growth and emotional healing. Embrace change and let go of all those things that no longer serve your needs.

Prioritize Emotional Healing: Consider engaging in activities that promote emotional healing and self-discovery. By focusing on your emotional well-being, you will enhance your overall health and create a more balanced and fulfilling life.

November: Focusing on Relationships

Overview

November is a month to focus on relationships, Aries. With the Sun in Sagittarius, there is an emphasis on personal connections and partnerships. This is a time to strengthen your relationships and create harmony in your interactions with others.

Key Dates

November 1: Full Moon in Taurus – Highlighting finances and material security.

November 10: Venus enters Sagittarius – Encouraging adventure and exploration in relationships.

November 23: New Moon in Sagittarius – A time for new beginnings in relationships and personal growth.

Detailed Horoscope

Full Moon in Taurus (November 1)

The Full Moon in Taurus on November 1 highlights your finances and material security. This lunar event activates your second house of money and possessions, urging you to assess your financial situation and make necessary adjustments to achieve your financial goals. Consider taking a closer look at your spending habits and making changes to enhance your financial stability.

With the Full Moon illuminating your second house, you are encouraged to focus on your financial well-being and create a sense of material security. Consider setting clear, ambitious goals for your finances and taking proactive steps towards achieving them. Your natural determination and practicality will help you attract positive financial opportunities and support from others.

The Full Moon in Taurus also highlights the importance of balance and stability in your financial life. You may find yourself reassessing your financial goals and making necessary adjustments to create a more balanced and secure financial future. Strive for a balance between your financial ambitions and your overall well-being.

Venus Enters Sagittarius (November 10)

Venus enters Sagittarius on November 10, bringing a focus on adventure and exploration in relationships. This transit activates your ninth house of travel and higher learning, encouraging you to embrace new experiences and expand your horizons in your relationships. Whether it's through travel, education, or spiritual pursuits, now is the time to explore new possibilities and create meaningful connections.

Venus in Sagittarius enhances your ability to connect with others on a deeper level and embrace new experiences. This is a time to focus on adventure and exploration in your relationships. Consider engaging in activities that promote personal growth and mutual understanding, such as travel, education, or spiritual pursuits.

The transit of Venus through Sagittarius also highlights the importance of openness and honesty in your interactions with others. Consider embracing new experiences and exploring new possibilities in your relationships. By being open and honest, you will enhance your relationships and create a sense of mutual understanding and respect.

New Moon in Sagittarius (November 23)

The New Moon on November 23 is a time for new beginnings in relationships and personal growth. This lunar event activates your ninth house of travel and higher learning, providing a fresh start for your personal growth and relationships. Use this energy to set new intentions and take proactive steps towards embracing new experiences and expanding your horizons.

With the New Moon illuminating your ninth house, you are encouraged to focus on personal growth and exploration. Consider setting new intentions related to your relationships, travel, and higher learning. Your efforts to embrace new experiences and expand your horizons will pay off in the long run, enhancing your overall well-being.

The New Moon in Sagittarius also highlights the importance of adventure and exploration in your relationships. Consider engaging in activities that promote personal growth and mutual understanding, such as travel, education, or spiritual pursuits. By embracing new experiences and exploring new possibilities, you will create stronger, more fulfilling relationships.

Practical Tips for November

Focus on Finances: Use the energy of the Full Moon in Taurus to assess your financial situation and make necessary adjustments to achieve your financial goals. Create a sense of material security and stability.

Embrace Adventure: With Venus in Sagittarius, focus on adventure and exploration in your relationships. Engage in activities that promote personal growth and mutual understanding.

Set Relationship Goals: Use the energy of the New Moon in Sagittarius to set new intentions for your relationships and personal growth.

Embrace new experiences and expand your horizons.

Be Open and Honest: Focus on openness and honesty in your interactions with others. By being open and honest, you will enhance your relationships and create a sense of mutual understanding and respect.

December: Embracing New Opportunities

Overview

December brings new opportunities for growth and expansion, Aries. With the Sun in Capricorn, there is a focus on career and long-term goals. This is a time to embrace new experiences and pursue your ambitions with determination.

Key Dates

December 1: Full Moon in Gemini – Highlighting communication and social connections.

December 10: Mercury enters Capricorn – Encouraging practical communication and strategic planning.

December 23: New Moon in Capricorn – A time for new beginnings in career and long-term goals.

Detailed Horoscope

Full Moon in Gemini (December 1)

The Full Moon in Gemini on December 1 highlights your communication and social connections. This lunar event activates your third house of communication and community, urging you to strengthen your relationships and engage in activities that enhance your communication skills. Consider reaching out to friends, networking, or participating in community events to expand your social circle.

With the Full Moon illuminating your third house, you are encouraged to focus on your communication skills and social connections. Consider setting clear, ambitious goals for your communication and networking efforts. Your natural charisma and ability to connect with others will help you attract positive attention and support from others.

The Full Moon in Gemini also highlights the importance of balance and clarity in your communication. You may find yourself reassessing your communication style and making necessary adjustments to create more effective and meaningful interactions. Strive for a balance between your personal goals and your ability to connect with others.

Mercury Enters Capricorn (December 10)

Mercury enters Capricorn on December 10, bringing a focus on practical communication and strategic planning. This transit activates your tenth house of career and public life, encouraging you to take a practical approach to your professional goals and create a clear plan for achieving your ambitions. Whether it's through strategic planning, networking, or seeking professional advice, now is the time to focus on your career and long-term goals.

Mercury in Capricorn enhances your ability to communicate with clarity and precision. This is a time to focus on practical communication and strategic planning in your professional life. Consider engaging in activities that promote your career goals, such as networking, seeking professional advice, or creating a clear plan for your future.

The transit of Mercury through Capricorn also highlights the importance of discipline and determination in achieving your goals. Consider setting clear, ambitious goals for your career and taking proactive steps towards achieving them. Your natural determination and practicality will help you attract positive opportunities and support from others.

New Moon in Capricorn (December 23)

The New Moon on December 23 is a time for new beginnings in career and long-term goals. This lunar event activates your tenth house of career and public life, providing a fresh start for your professional ambitions and personal goals. Use this energy to set new intentions and take proactive steps towards achieving your career and long-term goals.

With the New Moon illuminating your tenth house, you are encouraged to focus on your career and long-term goals. Consider setting new intentions related to your professional growth and personal ambitions. Your efforts to create a clear plan and take proactive steps towards your goals will pay off in the long run, enhancing your overall well-being.

The New Moon in Capricorn also highlights the importance of discipline and determination in achieving your goals. Consider engaging in activities that promote your career goals, such as networking, seeking professional advice, or creating a clear plan for your future. By staying focused and determined, you will create a more balanced and fulfilling life.

Practical Tips for December

Strengthen Communication: Use the energy of the Full Moon in Gemini to focus on your communication skills and social connections.

Seek out and engage in activities that enhance your communication skills and expand your social circle.

Focus on Career Goals: With Mercury in Capricorn, focus on practical communication and strategic planning in your professional life.

Create a clear plan and take proactive steps towards achieving your career goals. They are closer than you think.

Set Ambitious Goals: Use the energy of the New Moon in Capricorn to set new intentions for your career and long-term goals. Embrace discipline and focus in pursuit of your ambitions and you can turn dreams into reality.

Stay Focused and Determined: Focus on discipline and determination in achieving your goals. By staying focused and determined, you will create a more balanced and fulfilling life.

If you found this book helpful, you can find Serena's daily horoscopes exclusively at **yourdailyfreehoroscope.com**

Printed in Great Britain
by Amazon

59735212R00037